I would like to dedicate my book to my CHILDREN...If you are passionate about something, find a way to share it with the rest of the world.

I would like to dedicate my book to my brother TROY DAVIDSON, Illustrator...Thank you for illustrating my book for me. Because of you, I am very proud of my first published book *If I Had A Wish*. Thank you for being a part of my project! I am very fortunate and appreciate you so much.

I would like to dedicate my book to my friend JENNI GEISER, my graphic designer and assistant...Thank you so much for all your hard work! I could not have done this without you. I appreciate you walking me through this adventure and supporting me through this process.

I would like to dedicate this book to my little friend LAURYN...Don't grow up too fast. As you grow...use your imagination, make memories and tell your stories. May all your wishes come true!

Lastly, I would like to dedicate my book to "RIPPLES OF KINDNESS". Please check out the website. When I wrote my books, I not only wanted to inspire children to rhyme and accomplish personal goals, I also wanted to pay it forward. I hope *If I Had A Wish* and all my future books can bring awareness to Ripples of Kindness.

www.ripplesofkindness.com

T.C sillyspree will be donating a portion of the books proceeds to Ripples of Kindness.

If I Had A Wish

Copyright © 2011 by Teresa Campbell

All rights reserved.

www.tcsillyspree.com

ISBN-13: 978-1478338949

ISBN-10: 1478338946

Edited by createspace

First Edition

IF I HAD A WISH... I would wish for a snow day.
No daycare, no school. Now that would be cool.

I could swim all day in my indoor pool.

Build a fort and watch my favorite sport.

Or read a book and sit in my nook.

Then take a nap in my dog's lap.
I don't get too many days like this. Overall it's been bliss.

IF I HAD A WISH... I would wish I could travel in time.
I would want you to come along, if it was just me it would feel wrong.

There will be so much to see. So many different places to be.
We could stay long enough to play, or we could stay the whole day.

We'd go many different places and see many different faces.
A time machine would be pretty keen.

IF I HAD A WISH... I would wish for a money tree.
Maybe instead of one, I would plant three.

I would never have to worry about paying a fee.
I would grow so much money, I would hardly be able to see.

I would save some in my piggy bank. Even hide some behind my fish tank.
I would spend some on you and me. Maybe even buy another tree.
Money tree plus three... whew!

IF I HAD A WISH...
I would wish for one more day with my pets in heaven.
Matter of fact, I think I have seven.

I would cuddle with them, snuggle with them, hug them and love them!
I would treasure this day, I'd have them to play.

I am not confused, I know where they stay.
They're loved by their other friends in Heaven.
That's why I'd give them back, all seven!

IF I HAD A WISH... I would wish I could fly.
I would fly high, at least I would try.

I would fly low, and slow.
I would fly fast, blast past.

I would fly up and down, weave all around
At least until you said, "Get back on the ground!"

IF I HAD A WISH...
I'd wish I could snap my fingers and make anything appear.
Call me crazy! I know that seems lazy.

SNAP... I'm dressed, ready to impress.

SNAP... Eggs and toast,
a little later we'll snap a roast.

SNAP... I want a snack,
GOSH, I'm feeling like a slack!

SNAP... Mac & cheese,
SNAP... a little more please.

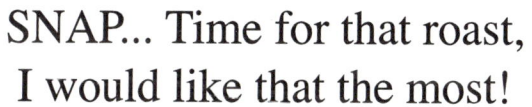

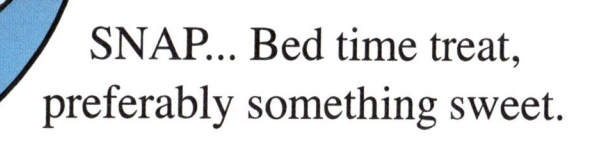

SNAP... Time for that roast,
I would like that the most!

SNAP... Bed time treat,
preferably something sweet.

Snap... jammies on. Goodnight everyone!

IF I HAD A WISH...
I'd wish for a day at the fair.

I love to sample all the food!
I'd eat so much you'd think it was rude.

I love Ferris wheels, roller coasters, and merry-go-rounds.
We could even just walk around the fair grounds.

I can hear all
of the different sounds:

Giggling, walking,
squealing, screaming...

So many people,
they are all beaming.

IF I HAD A WISH... I would wish for another wish.
I would have two. One wish I would wish for something new.
The other would be for something to do.

That something new just might be blue.
That something to do would be with I don't know who.
Maybe it won't be with a who, instead with a kangaroo.

Everyone will say "Lucky you"!

I have wished plenty. It's your turn to come up with a wish.
If you come upon a well, think of your wish, but don't tell.
Close your eyes, come up with something wise.

Imagine it true
and just as you do...
that's your cue.

Toss in your penny
along with the many.

Now, all you have to do
is wait for that wish to come true.

When my kids were at an age where they required a little less of mom, I began exploring what else may interest me outside of being a mother and a hairdresser. I opened my mind and heart and discovered that I really like rhyming and writing children's poetry.

Rhyming made me laugh which inspired me to do it more. When I'm writing my books, I don't think too much about what I'm writing, I just let my imagination do the work. I write about things that I relate to, from childhood memories to experiences that I've had as a mom and as an adult.

Being able to create, imagine, and inspire others is something that I do not take for granted. I love to tell familiar stories and create new ones. I hope *If I Had A Wish* helps you to reflect on your own wishes, challenges your imagination and inspires you to share your stories too.
- T.C. Sillyspree

I am currently an eighth grade English teacher in Annandale, Minnesota. In my spare time I like to ride my motorcycle, read, write, and draw. I would like to dedicate my illustrations to my awesome little buddy, my son Parker, who is six years old and starting kindergarten this year.
- Troy Davidson, Illustrator

Judy

May all your wishes come true!

T. L. Silly Spree

Best Wishes!